50 Quick Breakfast for Busy Mornings Recipes for Summer

By: Kelly Johnson

Table of Contents

- Overnight Oats with Berries
- Greek Yogurt Parfait with Granola
- Smoothie Bowl with Spinach and Banana
- Avocado Toast with Poached Egg
- Peanut Butter Banana Smoothie
- Egg Muffins with Vegetables
- Chia Seed Pudding with Almond Milk
- Breakfast Burritos with Eggs and Salsa
- Fruit Salad with Honey and Lime
- Mini Quiches with Spinach and Cheese
- Cottage Cheese with Pineapple and Nuts
- Granola Bars with Dried Fruits
- Quick Oatmeal with Maple Syrup
- Savory Breakfast Bowls with Quinoa
- Breakfast Smoothie with Protein Powder
- Rice Cakes with Hummus and Veggies
- Homemade Breakfast Sandwiches
- Fruit and Nut Overnight Chia Pudding
- Instant Oatmeal Cups with Cinnamon
- Peach and Yogurt Parfait
- Veggie Wraps with Scrambled Eggs
- Nut Butter and Banana Rice Cakes
- Cereal with Fresh Berries
- Egg and Avocado Toast
- Mini Pancakes with Maple Syrup
- Smoothie with Spinach, Mango, and Almond Milk
- Quinoa Breakfast Bowl with Almonds
- Cold Brew Coffee with Oat Milk
- Breakfast Tacos with Eggs and Salsa
- Apple Slices with Nut Butter

- Cucumber and Cream Cheese Sandwiches
- Muesli with Yogurt and Honey
- Breakfast Pizza with Eggs and Veggies
- Egg and Spinach Wraps
- Frozen Yogurt Bark with Fruits
- Quick Veggie Stir-Fry with Eggs
- Banana Oatmeal Cookies
- Zucchini Fritters with Yogurt Dip
- Coconut Yogurt with Berries
- Breakfast Quesadilla with Cheese
- Avocado and Tomato Salad
- Protein Bars with Nuts and Seeds
- Savory Oatmeal with Cheese and Herbs
- Instant Smoothie Packs for Blending
- Fruit and Yogurt Smoothie
- Egg Salad Lettuce Wraps
- Oatmeal Pancakes with Blueberries
- Honey and Almond Butter Toast
- Banana and Oat Smoothie
- Vegetable Frittata Muffins

Overnight Oats with Berries

Ingredients

- 1 cup rolled oats
- 1 cup almond milk
- 1/2 cup mixed berries (strawberries, blueberries, raspberries)
- 1 tablespoon honey or maple syrup
- 1 tablespoon chia seeds (optional)

Instructions

1. In a jar or bowl, combine rolled oats, almond milk, honey, and chia seeds.
2. Stir well, cover, and refrigerate overnight.
3. In the morning, top with mixed berries before serving.

Greek Yogurt Parfait with Granola

Ingredients

- 1 cup Greek yogurt
- 1/2 cup granola
- 1/2 cup fresh fruit (berries, banana, or peach)
- Honey for drizzling (optional)

Instructions

1. In a glass or bowl, layer Greek yogurt, granola, and fresh fruit.
2. Drizzle with honey if desired, and serve immediately.

Smoothie Bowl with Spinach and Banana

Ingredients

- 1 banana, frozen
- 1 cup spinach
- 1/2 cup almond milk
- Toppings: sliced banana, chia seeds, and granola

Instructions

1. In a blender, combine frozen banana, spinach, and almond milk. Blend until smooth.
2. Pour into a bowl and top with sliced banana, chia seeds, and granola.

Avocado Toast with Poached Egg

Ingredients

- 2 slices whole-grain bread
- 1 ripe avocado
- 2 eggs
- Salt and pepper to taste
- Optional toppings: red pepper flakes, feta cheese, or microgreens

Instructions

1. Toast the bread slices.
2. Mash the avocado and spread it on the toast, seasoning with salt and pepper.
3. Poach the eggs and place them on top of the avocado toast. Add optional toppings if desired.

Peanut Butter Banana Smoothie

Ingredients

- 1 banana
- 2 tablespoons peanut butter
- 1 cup almond milk
- 1 tablespoon honey (optional)

Instructions

1. In a blender, combine banana, peanut butter, almond milk, and honey. Blend until smooth.
2. Pour into a glass and enjoy immediately.

Egg Muffins with Vegetables

Ingredients

- 6 eggs
- 1/2 cup diced vegetables (bell peppers, spinach, onions)
- Salt and pepper to taste
- Optional: cheese for topping

Instructions

1. Preheat the oven to 350°F (175°C).
2. In a bowl, whisk together the eggs, salt, and pepper.
3. Stir in diced vegetables.
4. Pour the mixture into a greased muffin tin and bake for 20-25 minutes, until set.

Chia Seed Pudding with Almond Milk

Ingredients

- 1/4 cup chia seeds
- 1 cup almond milk
- 1 tablespoon honey or maple syrup (optional)
- Toppings: fresh fruit, nuts, or granola

Instructions

1. In a jar or bowl, combine chia seeds, almond milk, and honey.
2. Stir well, cover, and refrigerate for at least 4 hours or overnight.
3. Serve with your choice of toppings.

Let me know if you need more recipes or adjustments!

Breakfast Burritos with Eggs and Salsa

Ingredients

- 4 large eggs
- 1/2 cup shredded cheese (cheddar or your choice)
- 1/2 cup salsa
- 4 large tortillas
- Salt and pepper to taste

Instructions

1. In a bowl, whisk together the eggs, salt, and pepper.
2. Scramble the eggs in a skillet over medium heat until cooked.
3. Assemble each burrito by placing scrambled eggs, cheese, and salsa on a tortilla, rolling it up tightly.

Fruit Salad with Honey and Lime

Ingredients

- 2 cups mixed fresh fruit (strawberries, melon, grapes, kiwi)
- 1 tablespoon honey
- Juice of 1 lime

Instructions

1. In a large bowl, combine mixed fruit.
2. Drizzle with honey and lime juice, tossing gently to combine. Serve chilled.

Mini Quiches with Spinach and Cheese

Ingredients

- 6 eggs
- 1 cup fresh spinach, chopped
- 1/2 cup shredded cheese (Swiss or cheddar)
- Salt and pepper to taste
- 1/2 cup milk

Instructions

1. Preheat the oven to 350°F (175°C).
2. In a bowl, whisk together the eggs, milk, salt, and pepper.
3. Stir in spinach and cheese.
4. Pour the mixture into greased muffin tins and bake for 20-25 minutes until set.

Cottage Cheese with Pineapple and Nuts

Ingredients

- 1 cup cottage cheese
- 1/2 cup pineapple chunks (fresh or canned)
- 1/4 cup mixed nuts (almonds, walnuts, or pecans)

Instructions

1. In a bowl, combine cottage cheese, pineapple chunks, and mixed nuts.
2. Serve immediately as a refreshing breakfast.

Granola Bars with Dried Fruits

Ingredients

- 2 cups rolled oats
- 1 cup honey or maple syrup
- 1/2 cup nut butter (peanut or almond)
- 1 cup dried fruits (raisins, cranberries, or apricots)

Instructions

1. Preheat the oven to 350°F (175°C) and line a baking dish with parchment paper.
2. In a bowl, mix oats, honey, nut butter, and dried fruits until combined.
3. Press the mixture into the baking dish and bake for 15-20 minutes.
4. Let cool before cutting into bars.

Quick Oatmeal with Maple Syrup

Ingredients

- 1 cup quick oats
- 2 cups water or milk
- 2 tablespoons maple syrup
- Optional toppings: nuts, fruit, or cinnamon

Instructions

1. In a saucepan, bring water or milk to a boil.
2. Stir in oats and reduce heat, cooking for 1-2 minutes until thickened.
3. Sweeten with maple syrup and add desired toppings before serving.

Savory Breakfast Bowls with Quinoa

Ingredients

- 1 cup cooked quinoa
- 2 eggs, cooked to your preference (poached or fried)
- 1/2 avocado, sliced
- 1/2 cup sautéed vegetables (spinach, bell peppers, or mushrooms)
- Salt and pepper to taste

Instructions

1. In a bowl, layer cooked quinoa, topped with eggs, avocado, and sautéed vegetables.
2. Season with salt and pepper before serving.

Let me know if you need more recipes or adjustments!

Breakfast Smoothie with Protein Powder

Ingredients

- 1 banana
- 1 cup spinach
- 1 scoop protein powder (vanilla or chocolate)
- 1 cup almond milk (or milk of choice)
- 1 tablespoon peanut butter (optional)

Instructions

1. In a blender, combine the banana, spinach, protein powder, almond milk, and peanut butter.
2. Blend until smooth and creamy. Serve immediately.

Rice Cakes with Hummus and Veggies

Ingredients

- 4 rice cakes
- 1 cup hummus
- 1 cup assorted vegetables (cucumber, bell peppers, carrots)

Instructions

1. Spread hummus generously over each rice cake.
2. Top with sliced vegetables. Serve as a quick breakfast or snack.

Homemade Breakfast Sandwiches

Ingredients

- 4 eggs
- 4 slices of cheese (cheddar or your choice)
- 4 English muffins or bagels
- 4 slices of cooked bacon or sausage patties

Instructions

1. Cook the eggs to your preference (fried or scrambled).
2. Toast the English muffins or bagels.
3. Assemble each sandwich with an egg, cheese, and bacon or sausage.

Fruit and Nut Overnight Chia Pudding

Ingredients

- 1/4 cup chia seeds
- 1 cup almond milk (or milk of choice)
- 1 tablespoon honey or maple syrup
- 1/2 cup mixed fruits (berries, banana)
- 1/4 cup nuts (almonds or walnuts)

Instructions

1. In a bowl, mix chia seeds, almond milk, and sweetener.
2. Cover and refrigerate overnight.
3. Serve topped with mixed fruits and nuts in the morning.

Instant Oatmeal Cups with Cinnamon

Ingredients

- 2 cups rolled oats
- 1/4 cup brown sugar
- 1 teaspoon cinnamon
- 1/2 cup dried fruits (raisins, cranberries)
- 4 cups water or milk

Instructions

1. In a bowl, mix oats, brown sugar, cinnamon, and dried fruits.
2. Divide into cups.
3. To prepare, add boiling water or milk and let sit for 3-5 minutes before eating.

Peach and Yogurt Parfait

Ingredients

- 2 cups yogurt (plain or flavored)
- 2 ripe peaches, diced
- 1/2 cup granola

Instructions

1. In a glass or bowl, layer yogurt, diced peaches, and granola.
2. Repeat the layers until all ingredients are used. Serve immediately.

Veggie Wraps with Scrambled Eggs

Ingredients

- 4 large tortillas
- 4 eggs
- 1 cup mixed vegetables (bell peppers, spinach, onions)
- Salt and pepper to taste

Instructions

1. Scramble eggs in a skillet with mixed vegetables, seasoning with salt and pepper.
2. Fill each tortilla with the scrambled egg mixture, rolling it up tightly. Serve warm.

Let me know if you need more recipes or adjustments!

Nut Butter and Banana Rice Cakes

Ingredients

- 4 rice cakes
- 1/2 cup nut butter (peanut, almond, or cashew)
- 1 banana, sliced

Instructions

1. Spread nut butter evenly over each rice cake.
2. Top with banana slices and serve immediately.

Cereal with Fresh Berries

Ingredients

- 2 cups your favorite cereal
- 1 cup milk (dairy or non-dairy)
- 1 cup fresh berries (strawberries, blueberries, raspberries)

Instructions

1. In a bowl, add cereal and pour milk over it.
2. Top with fresh berries and enjoy.

Egg and Avocado Toast

Ingredients

- 2 slices whole-grain bread
- 2 eggs
- 1 avocado
- Salt and pepper to taste

Instructions

1. Toast the bread slices.
2. In a skillet, cook eggs to your preference (poached, fried, or scrambled).
3. Mash avocado and spread it on toast, topping it with the cooked eggs. Season with salt and pepper.

Mini Pancakes with Maple Syrup

Ingredients

- 1 cup pancake mix
- 3/4 cup water
- Maple syrup for serving

Instructions

1. In a bowl, mix pancake mix with water until combined.
2. Heat a skillet over medium heat and pour small amounts of batter to form mini pancakes. Cook until bubbles form, then flip and cook until golden brown.
3. Serve warm with maple syrup.

Smoothie with Spinach, Mango, and Almond Milk

Ingredients

- 1 cup fresh spinach
- 1 cup frozen mango chunks
- 1 cup almond milk
- 1 tablespoon honey (optional)

Instructions

1. In a blender, combine spinach, mango, almond milk, and honey.
2. Blend until smooth and serve immediately.

Quinoa Breakfast Bowl with Almonds

Ingredients

- 1 cup cooked quinoa
- 1/4 cup almonds, chopped
- 1 tablespoon honey or maple syrup
- 1/2 cup fresh fruit (berries or sliced banana)

Instructions

1. In a bowl, combine cooked quinoa, almonds, and honey.
2. Top with fresh fruit and serve warm.

Cold Brew Coffee with Oat Milk

Ingredients

- 1 cup cold brew coffee
- 1/2 cup oat milk
- Sweetener of choice (optional)

Instructions

1. In a glass, combine cold brew coffee and oat milk.
2. Stir in sweetener if desired and enjoy chilled.

Let me know if you need more recipes or any modifications!

Breakfast Tacos with Eggs and Salsa

Ingredients

- 4 small tortillas
- 4 eggs
- 1/2 cup salsa
- 1/2 cup shredded cheese (optional)

Instructions

1. Scramble the eggs in a skillet until fully cooked.
2. Fill each tortilla with scrambled eggs, top with salsa and cheese if desired. Serve warm.

Apple Slices with Nut Butter

Ingredients

- 2 apples, sliced
- 1/2 cup nut butter (peanut, almond, or cashew)

Instructions

1. Arrange apple slices on a plate.
2. Serve with nut butter for dipping.

Cucumber and Cream Cheese Sandwiches

Ingredients

- 1 cucumber, sliced
- 4 ounces cream cheese
- 4 slices whole-grain bread

Instructions

1. Spread cream cheese on each slice of bread.
2. Layer cucumber slices on top and close the sandwiches. Cut into quarters and serve.

Muesli with Yogurt and Honey

Ingredients

- 1 cup muesli
- 1 cup yogurt (plain or flavored)
- 1 tablespoon honey

Instructions

1. In a bowl, layer muesli and yogurt.
2. Drizzle honey on top and mix before eating.

Breakfast Pizza with Eggs and Veggies

Ingredients

- 1 pre-made pizza crust
- 4 eggs
- 1 cup assorted vegetables (bell peppers, spinach, onions)
- 1/2 cup shredded cheese

Instructions

1. Preheat the oven according to pizza crust instructions.
2. Spread vegetables on the pizza crust, crack eggs on top, and sprinkle cheese.
3. Bake according to crust instructions until eggs are set. Slice and serve.

Egg and Spinach Wraps

Ingredients

- 4 large tortillas
- 4 eggs
- 2 cups fresh spinach
- Salt and pepper to taste

Instructions

1. In a skillet, scramble the eggs with spinach, seasoning with salt and pepper.
2. Fill each tortilla with the egg and spinach mixture, rolling them up tightly. Serve warm.

Frozen Yogurt Bark with Fruits

Ingredients

- 2 cups yogurt (plain or flavored)
- 1 cup mixed fruits (berries, banana, kiwi)
- 1/4 cup granola (optional)

Instructions

1. Spread yogurt evenly on a parchment-lined baking sheet.
2. Top with mixed fruits and granola. Freeze for at least 2 hours, then break into pieces and serve.

Let me know if you need more recipes or adjustments!

Quick Veggie Stir-Fry with Eggs

Ingredients

- 2 cups mixed vegetables (bell peppers, broccoli, carrots)
- 4 eggs
- 2 tablespoons soy sauce
- 1 tablespoon olive oil

Instructions

1. In a skillet, heat olive oil over medium heat and add mixed vegetables. Stir-fry until tender.
2. Push the veggies to one side, crack in the eggs, and scramble until cooked. Add soy sauce, mix well, and serve.

Banana Oatmeal Cookies

Ingredients

- 2 ripe bananas, mashed
- 1 cup oats
- 1/2 teaspoon cinnamon (optional)
- 1/4 cup chocolate chips (optional)

Instructions

1. Preheat the oven to 350°F (175°C).
2. In a bowl, mix mashed bananas with oats and cinnamon. Stir in chocolate chips if using.
3. Drop spoonfuls of the mixture onto a baking sheet and bake for 10-12 minutes until set.

Zucchini Fritters with Yogurt Dip

Ingredients

- 2 cups grated zucchini
- 1/2 cup flour
- 2 eggs
- Salt and pepper to taste
- 1 cup plain yogurt (for dipping)

Instructions

1. In a bowl, mix grated zucchini, flour, eggs, salt, and pepper until combined.
2. Heat a skillet over medium heat, spoon batter to form fritters, and cook until golden brown on both sides. Serve with yogurt dip.

Coconut Yogurt with Berries

Ingredients

- 1 cup coconut yogurt
- 1 cup mixed berries (strawberries, blueberries, raspberries)
- 1 tablespoon honey or maple syrup (optional)

Instructions

1. In a bowl, layer coconut yogurt and top with mixed berries.
2. Drizzle with honey or maple syrup if desired and serve.

Breakfast Quesadilla with Cheese

Ingredients

- 2 tortillas
- 1 cup shredded cheese (cheddar, mozzarella, or your choice)
- Optional: cooked eggs, beans, or veggies

Instructions

1. Heat a skillet over medium heat and place one tortilla in it.
2. Sprinkle cheese (and any optional fillings) on top, then place the second tortilla over it. Cook until golden brown, flipping halfway. Cut into wedges and serve.

Avocado and Tomato Salad

Ingredients

- 2 ripe avocados, diced
- 2 cups cherry tomatoes, halved
- 2 tablespoons olive oil
- Salt and pepper to taste

Instructions

1. In a bowl, combine diced avocado and cherry tomatoes.
2. Drizzle with olive oil, season with salt and pepper, and toss gently before serving.

Protein Bars with Nuts and Seeds

Ingredients

- 1 cup mixed nuts (almonds, walnuts, cashews)
- 1/2 cup seeds (chia, sunflower, pumpkin)
- 1 cup protein powder
- 1/2 cup honey or maple syrup

Instructions

1. In a large bowl, mix all ingredients until well combined.
2. Press the mixture into a lined baking dish and refrigerate until firm. Cut into bars and serve.

Let me know if you need more recipes or adjustments!

Savory Oatmeal with Cheese and Herbs

Ingredients

- 1 cup rolled oats
- 2 cups water or broth
- 1/2 cup shredded cheese (cheddar or your choice)
- 1 tablespoon chopped fresh herbs (such as chives or parsley)
- Salt and pepper to taste

Instructions

1. In a saucepan, bring water or broth to a boil. Add oats and cook according to package instructions.
2. Stir in cheese, herbs, salt, and pepper before serving.

Instant Smoothie Packs for Blending

Ingredients

- 1 cup mixed fruit (frozen berries, banana, spinach)
- 1/2 cup yogurt or milk of choice
- 1 tablespoon protein powder (optional)

Instructions

1. Divide the fruit and yogurt into individual freezer bags.
2. When ready to blend, add the contents to a blender with your choice of milk and blend until smooth.

Fruit and Yogurt Smoothie

Ingredients

- 1 cup yogurt
- 1 cup mixed fruit (fresh or frozen)
- 1 tablespoon honey (optional)

Instructions

1. Combine yogurt, mixed fruit, and honey in a blender.
2. Blend until smooth and serve immediately.

Egg Salad Lettuce Wraps

Ingredients

- 4 hard-boiled eggs, chopped
- 2 tablespoons mayonnaise
- 1 teaspoon mustard
- Salt and pepper to taste
- Lettuce leaves for wrapping

Instructions

1. In a bowl, mix chopped eggs, mayonnaise, mustard, salt, and pepper.
2. Serve the egg salad in lettuce leaves as wraps.

Oatmeal Pancakes with Blueberries

Ingredients

- 1 cup rolled oats
- 1 cup milk
- 1 egg
- 1 cup blueberries
- 1 teaspoon baking powder

Instructions

1. In a bowl, mix oats, milk, egg, and baking powder until combined.
2. Fold in blueberries. Cook pancakes on a hot skillet until golden brown on both sides.

Honey and Almond Butter Toast

Ingredients

- 2 slices whole-grain bread
- 2 tablespoons almond butter
- 1 tablespoon honey
- Sliced banana or apple (optional)

Instructions

1. Toast the bread slices.
2. Spread almond butter on top, drizzle with honey, and add fruit slices if desired.

Banana and Oat Smoothie

Ingredients

- 1 ripe banana
- 1/2 cup rolled oats
- 1 cup milk or plant-based milk
- 1 tablespoon honey (optional)

Instructions

1. In a blender, combine banana, oats, milk, and honey.
2. Blend until smooth and serve.

Vegetable Frittata Muffins

Ingredients

- 6 eggs
- 1 cup chopped vegetables (bell peppers, spinach, onions)
- 1/2 cup shredded cheese
- Salt and pepper to taste

Instructions

1. Preheat the oven to 350°F (175°C). Grease a muffin tin.
2. In a bowl, whisk together eggs, vegetables, cheese, salt, and pepper.
3. Pour the mixture into muffin tins and bake for 15-20 minutes until set.

Let me know if you need more recipes or any adjustments!

www.ingramcontent.com/pod-product-compliance
Lightning Source LLC
LaVergne TN
LVHW081501060526
838201LV00056BA/2878